THE LOWESTOFT TRAIN
BY
MALCOLM WHITE

Coastal and Maritime Heritage Series
2002

INFORMATION

Published by   Malcolm R. White
Coastal Publications
71 Beeching Drive
Lowestoft, NR32 4TB
England, UK

Printed by   Microspress Printers Ltd.
27 Norwich Road
Halesworth
Suffolk, IP19 8BX
England, UK

First Published   June 2002
Second Impression   August 2002
Third Impression   November 2003
Copyright ©   Malcolm R. White 2002

ISBN 0 9532485 6 9

All rights reserved.

Every effort has been made to ensure the information in this book is accurate. For this reason, official documentation, various research works and local records have been consulted for factual support. Some of this information is attributable to other parties. Minutes of meetings of the Eastern Counties Railway, Great Eastern Railway and the London and North Eastern Railway have been consulted, and information drawn from these incorporated in this work. As with other works in this series, all measurements and distances are stated in British Imperial. Books in this series are part of the National Published Archive, and are included in the library collections of the British Library, the National Library of Scotland, the National Library of Wales, the Universities of Oxford and Cambridge and that of Trinity College, Dublin.

FRONT COVER PHOTOGRAPH

The "Easterling", a popular named train, was scheduled to run non-stop between London Liverpool Street and Beccles, where the train divided into two sections. One section went to Lowestoft Central and the other to Yarmouth Southtown. Leaving Liverpool Street at 10.33 am, the "Easterling" was scheduled to arrive at Lowestoft at 1.24pm. A regular performer on the East Suffolk line, Class B17/6 4-6-0 No. 61669 *Barnsley*, is seen heading the train through pleasant north Suffolk countryside in July 1957. *Barnsley* was a long time resident of Ipswich shed and was withdrawn from service in 1958. It was scrapped at Doncaster Works in November of that year.

TITLE PAGE PHOTOGRAPH

From the family album A splendid scene in Great Eastern Railway days at Lowestoft with a clean GER Class S46 4-4-0 No. 1863 on shed and members of the locomotive crew and shed personnel, including a relation of the author, posing for the camera. Under the LNER this locomotive became Class D14 No. 8863 and after being modified a number of times was eventually scrapped, as Class D16/3 No. 62534, having been withdrawn from Cambridge Shed in October 1958.

OPPOSITE PAGE PHOTOGRAPH

A scene on the East Suffolk Line in the mid 1960s as Brush Type 4 Co-Co diesel electric locomotive working the London Liverpool Street to Lowestoft through train accelerates away from Saxmundham. Typical features of this line at that time and visible here, include bay platforms, goods sidings, semaphore signals and track without grass and weeds! Introduced in 1962, and powered by a 12 cylinder 2750 hp Sulzer engine, the Brush Type 4 later became the Class 47 and were a familiar sight in East Anglia for many years hauling express passenger trains. In recent years many locomotives of this class have been scrapped.

CONTENTS

ACKNOWLEDGEMENTS

Without the support and assistance of many kind, enthusiastic and generous people interested in local railways, this comprehensive work would not have been possible. I am in particular grateful to Mr. Stuart Jones BA, Mr. Peter Killby, Mr. Peter Parker, Mr. G. Moore, Mr. David White, Mr. Steffan White, and Louise Clarke and the staff of the Suffolk Record Office for assistance in this complex research and local history project. As with other titles in this series, the Port of Lowestoft Research Society and the Lowestoft & East Suffolk Maritime Museum have contributed in many ways, including allowing access to and use of their archives and records relating to the railway and town. The use in this book of valuable archive material previously in the collections of the late Mr. Bill Harvey, Shedmaster at various locations including Norwich, and the late Mr. J. L. Simpson, Shedmaster at "Top Shed", Kings Cross in this book is greatly appreciated.

PHOTOGRAPHIC OWNERSHIP AND COPYRIGHT

Class WD 2-8-0 No 90001 at Oulton Broad North

Britannia Class 7MT 4-6-2 No. 70042 *Lord Roberts* at Ipswich

INTRODUCTION

From the middle of the 19th century, the railway at Lowestoft became the driving force for the development of the town, and provided a vital service to townsfolk, visitors, business, the port and industry. The town was very fortunate in having had such a major railway presence and much of the town's growth and prosperity could be attributed to the foresight of various railway engineers and builders. Few towns of comparative size could match the railway organisation, structure, number of lines and stations within the town boundary. Having a central station served by three different routes and providing excellent access to many parts of the country was a major advantage. In addition, the three other stations within the town boundary meant that as well as the town centre, other parts were well served.

Several railway engineering workshops, depots and facilities existed and provided much employment. A vast network of sidings and branch lines serving docks, factories and industrial premises developed around the town, in addition to the railway run harbour complete with a fleet of tugs, dredgers and miscellaneous vessels.

Railway companies have invested vast amounts of money locally and made major contributions to the town's economy. For some unknown reason this has been generally overlooked in the many local publications released over the years. I hope that this book will start to redress this, by highlighting, recording and reflecting upon the scenes around the railways of Lowestoft and the surrounding area. We briefly review the railway routes in the order in which they were opened, starting with the earliest, to Norwich, which opened in 1847. Lastly we review the railway scene within Lowestoft, the most easterly destination in the British Isles.

This book commemorates the 40th anniversary of the ending of timetabled steam traction on the railways of East Anglia.

Malcolm White
Lowestoft
June 2002

A railway network map, published before the First World War, of East Suffolk and Norfolk

A SCHEMATIC LAYOUT OF RAILWAY LINES IN CENTRAL LOWESTOFT IN THE 1950s

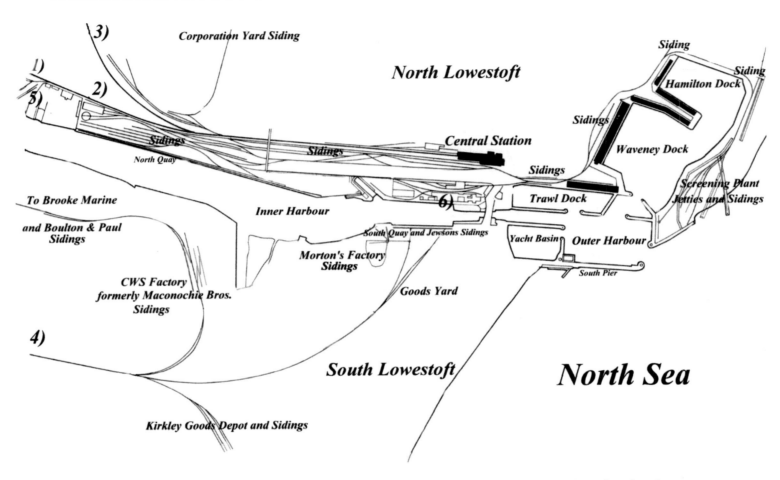

Please note that this diagram is not to scale, and does not indicate all the sidings at the various locations shown. In a few cases, sidings were of a temporary nature, and removed after fulfilling their use. The layout shown for Morton's factory, is as it was for Lucas Bros., the previous occupiers of the site.

Key
1) Line to Ipswich and Norwich   2) Locomotive shed and turntable   3) To Yarmouth Beach and Southtown
4) To Oulton Broad South and the East Suffolk Line   5) To Railway Sleeper Depot   6) Railway Harbour Works

THE RAILWAY APPROACHES TO LOWESTOFT IN THE 1920s

The map below shows the various railway lines in the area surrounding Lake Lothing in the late 1920s. At the bottom left corner, can be seen the harbour branch and the East Suffolk line converging on Oulton Broad South. Carlton Colville Swing Bridge, later renamed Oulton Broad Swing Bridge is seen, as is the new sleeper and creosoting depot, and Lowestoft locomotive depot and turntable. The Norfolk and Suffolk Joint Committee line to Yarmouth is quite prominent at the top right, after leaving Coke Ovens Junction in the centre right. Of note at the western end of Lake Lothing on the north shore are the sidings at Chambers No. 3 shipyard, and at the bottom right corner, the sidings of the Kirkley Goods Depot, and other lines of the extensive South Lowestoft harbour branch. This branch was extended and altered several times for access to various factories and other premises and these additions are not shown on this map. Please refer to the opposite page for further details.

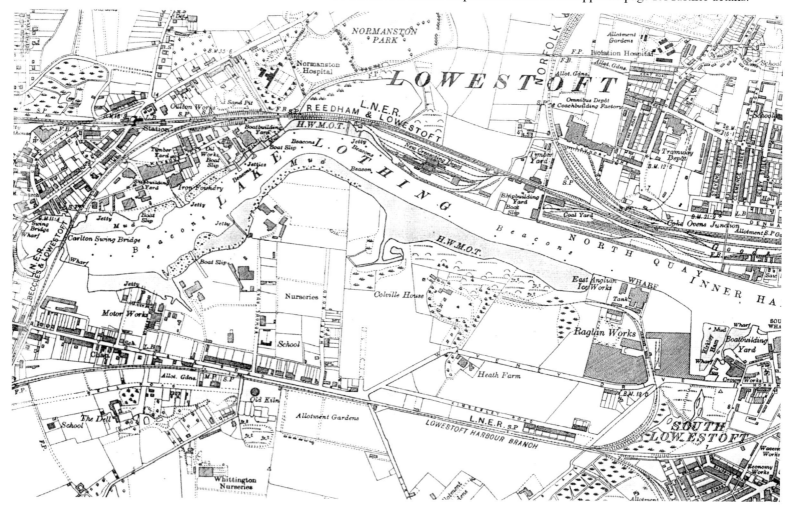

A SUMMARY OF THE RAILWAY AT LOWESTOFT

Before the coming of the railway Lowestoft relied heavily upon the sea and the waterways for the transportation of goods. The network of roads and cart tracks giving access to nearby villages and towns was basic with many hazards, often unseen, facing those who ventured to travel or send goods. The arrival of the railway was to revolutionise the way in which the population could travel from this most easterly point and, at the same time, gave easy and convenient accessibility to Lowestoft for the great masses throughout the land.

The development and expansion of the town, together with widening of the industrial base and the establishment of a buoyant tourist and holiday trade can be attributed to the railway. This new mode of travel enabled goods to be sent safety, swiftly and securely, and became very important to the local economy, at that time heavily reliant on the fishing trade. Fish could be sent by rail from Lowestoft and yet arrive fresh at many distant destinations. Vast quantities of coal, the driving force of industry, could be delivered by rail to the town to heat the boilers of the large fleet of drifters and trawlers; previously this had all arrived at the port by sea. Indeed, where would the town and the fishing industry have been without the railway companies to provide the necessary transport links and the harbour.

Regrettably, the long heavy goods and express fish trains at Lowestoft can no longer be witnessed. The lorry started to win the battle of how freight was to be moved many years ago, and today freight by rail has all but disappeared in the town. The passenger trains continue to provide an essential service to the resident, visitor and business interests, however the once popular through services provided by the Great Eastern and the Norfolk and Suffolk Joint Railways Committee routes, to such places as Birmingham, Derby, Leicester, Liverpool, Manchester, Sheffield and York are now mere memories. Many of these services had full restaurant facilities. In 2002, we have one long distance through train, this at present being provided by an Anglia Railways Class 170 diesel multiple unit travelling via the restrictive East Suffolk Line to London Liverpool Street.

DATES SIGNIFICANT TO THE RAILWAY WERE:-

1831   Lowestoft Harbour officially opened on the 10th August.

1832   Lowestoft Harbour completed.

1839   The first services were run by the Eastern Counties Railway (ECR) in the London area.

1843   At a meeting held in Lowestoft Town Hall, Mr. Samuel Morton Peto, a railway contractor, put forward proposals to build a railway that would enable fish landed at Lowestoft to be delivered fresh in Manchester.

1844   Samuel Morton Peto purchased the harbour from a syndicate of local businessmen for £12,500.

1845   The Lowestoft Railway and Harbour Company was formed. Having obtained the Act of Parliament, the improvement of the harbour and the building of a railway line from the town to Reedham could be planned. The Norwich and Brandon Railway Company in conjunction with the Yarmouth and Norwich Railway Company took out a lease in February on the Lowestoft Railway and Harbour Company and started to make improvements. Later the Yarmouth and Norwich Railway amalgamated with the Norfolk Railway, who then took over the lease. The first railway tug, the *Pursuit,* owned by the Norfolk Railway started work at the port.

1846   Construction of the railway and the infrastructure commenced.

1847   On the 3rd. May, the first train, consisting of goods wagons, ran from Lowestoft to Reedham, the line being leased and operated by the Norfolk Railway.

1848   Control of the railway and other interests at Lowestoft, including the harbour, was taken over by the ECR. Coke ovens required to produce the coke for firing their locomotives, were built at Lowestoft adjacent to the quay in the inner harbour where the coal used in the process was discharged from ships. The largest number of ovens in use at any one time was eighty-three. By the end of 1866, the ovens had been taken out of service and dismantled, coke having been replaced by coal as fuel for the locomotives.

1850   On the 29th. September it was officially announced that work had been completed on the railway and harbour. By that time, a new outer harbour had been created, formed by building two longer piers.

1851	The Halesworth, Beccles and Haddiscoe Railway (HBHR) was incorporated, and commenced building a line that would eventually link up with the Lowestoft - Reedham line at Haddiscoe.
1854	Upon the opening of their line in December, the HBHR became the East Suffolk Railway (ESR). Separate companies, which would later become part of the ESR, proposed a number of branch lines off the main route, and extension of the line from Beccles to Lowestoft and Haddiscoe to Yarmouth.
1855	A new Lowestoft station, replacing the original built in 1846-47, was completed by Lucas Bros. This firm, founded in 1847, was run by Charles and Thomas Lucas and later became well known as contractors, builders and developers. They were responsible for many major building projects locally, in London and elsewhere.
1856	By the end of the year, the Eastern Counties Railway had invested over £300, 000 in facilities at Lowestoft.
1857	Rates for the conveyance of Lowestoft fish to Manchester by the Lancashire and Yorkshire Railway were revised to 80/- per ton for fresh and 45/- for salted.
1858	The North of Europe Steam Navigation Company went into liquation.
1859	A number of new lines promoted by different companies opened on Wednesday 1st June, including those from Lowestoft to Beccles and Haddiscoe to Yarmouth. At Woodbridge, the ESR and a line built by the ECR from Ipswich joined, forming a direct line from Yarmouth and Lowestoft to Ipswich. The services over the new line were initially operated by the ECR. In addition, the Kirkley branch on the south side of the harbour at Lowestoft opened. During August, the ECR took over the harbour shearlegs and the cattle sheds from the North of Europe Steam Navigation Co. Commencing in July, large quantities of coal were sent to Yarmouth South Town via the Haddiscoe connection and the new East Suffolk Railway line. The former cattle sheds were occupied by various circus animals and also used by the Lowestoft Rifle Corps when empty.
1860	The collection of all tolls for shipping in the port was taken over by the Eastern Counties Railway. An instruction was issued by the railway authorities that all vessels seeking shelter in the port must do so in the Inner Harbour. Ownership of the stationmaster's house at Lowestoft was offered to the ECR. Due to serious delays encountered on the Great Northern Railway, the Manchester and Liverpool fish traffic was diverted to the London and North Western Railway.
1862	The Great Eastern Railway (GER) was formed. This was the result of the amalgamation of several companies including the East Suffolk and Eastern Counties Railways. The GER inherited the harbour at Lowestoft and also the Norwich and Lowestoft Navigation. Following the failure of the North of Europe Steam Navigation Company, their engineering works were taken over by the GER and became the railway Harbour Works.
1865	Fish market erected by the GER.
1875	A new paddle tug, the *Despatch* was built for the GER
1877	A new paddle tug, the *Rainbow*, was built for the GER for work at Parkeston Quay. She was transferred to Lowestoft in 1885.
1879	A new paddle tug, the *Imperial*, was built for the GER. This was the second paddle tug of that name to work at the port.
1882	Plans were announced for a new locomotive shed.
1883	The GER announced that plans had been drawn up for a new refreshment room at Lowestoft station. On the 1st October the new Herring and Mackerel Market and the Waveney Dock opened, both built by the GER. The first vessel into the dock was the company paddle tug *Despatch,* with a party of dignitaries on board. One of these was Lord Waveney, after whom the dock had been named.
1890	Casks of seawater were being dispatched by the GER to inland towns and cities for drinking. This service lasted until the 1930s.
1895	Development of the south side branch was agreed with Colville House Estates. A new level crossing to serve Maconochie Bros. cannery would be installed.
1898	1,215,000 sleepers were dispatched from the original Lowestoft sleeper depot during the five years ending 1897. The new twin screw tug *Lowestoft* entered service
1900	Plans were announced by the GER for a new shingle screening plant to be established at Lowestoft. A budget of £500 was set aside for the work.

1902	New swing bridges to be installed at Reedham costing £5591 and Somerleyton costing £9039.
1903	Doubling of the Lowestoft - Reedham line was undertaken. The third of Lowestoft's main railway links, the direct line between the town and Great Yarmouth, also opened on the 13th July. The Norfolk and Suffolk Joint Railways Committee, a combination of the GER and the Midland & Great Northern Joint Railway operated the line which was the third and shortest of three routes between the two towns. The first two both utilised part of the Lowestoft - Reedham line to gain access to existing lines converging on Yarmouth, albeit to different stations in the town. The first services ran via the Reedham East curve, which opened in 1847, and Berney Arms into Yarmouth Vauxhall; this was last used in 1926. Later, trains reached Yarmouth by joining the Beccles - Yarmouth Southtown line via the Marsh Junction - St. Olaves Swing Bridge spur, which had opened on the 1st June 1872.
1904	Cost of providing the shingle-screening plant amounted to £375. The GER commenced operating a bus service between Lowestoft, Kessingland and Southwold. They also had routes within the town. All were eventually taken over by United Automobile Services. The United was absorbed by the Eastern Counties Omnibus Co. Ltd. in 1931. A plan for a new bus garage was announced. It was decided on the 21st June, to construct a Kirkley Goods Yard. The land when acquired cost £3324.
1906	The garage to accommodate the GER buses based in the town was built in Denmark Road and cost £585. Another construction project, that of building the Hamilton Dock, reached completion and it was opened by Lord Claud Hamilton, chairman of the GER.
1908	New Carlton Colville (later Oulton Broad) Swing Bridge commissioned and in use by 19th May. The GER removed the previous old wooden structure.
1911	An extra siding was installed adjacent to the North Beach for collection of sand and shingle.
1913	Work commenced on a major new sleeper handling, processing, and distribution depot at Lowestoft on the north shore of Lake Lothing. Sheds were ordered for the site and Ransomes and Rapier were contracted to provide plant and machinery. This depot replaced the earlier one and cost £43,000 to set up. The Kirkley branch was extended with additional lines serving parts of south Lowestoft.
1917	The old sleeper depot was sold by the GER.
1919	Extra siding installed at Maconochie Bros. cannery.
1920	Major rail connected oil depot established at Oulton Broad by Anglo American Oil.
1921	Additional sidings authorised at Colby's shipyard, costing £976, and Maconochie Bros costing £3500.
1922	Contracts placed with A. Jackaman & Co. for rebuilding, adjacent to the shingle screening plant, a groyne for £3500 and building a new one for £6500.
1923	On the 1st January, the London and North Eastern Railway (LNER) came into being as an amalgamation of the Great Central, Great Eastern, Great Northern, North Eastern, North British and Great North of Scotland Railway companies. At Lowestoft, the LNER took over responsibility for the harbour and the shipping fleet.
1926	The Sentinel steam locomotives started work at Lowestoft
1929	Lowestoft Station was lit by electricity for the first time
1931	Mechanical coaling plant and new water plant installed at engine sheds. John Chamber's shipyard taken over by the LNER after being for sale since 1929.
1933	Thirteen shunting horses replaced by four tractors
1936	The last of the eleven railway paddle tugs to work at Lowestoft, the *Despatch* and *Imperial* were sold for scrapping.
1937	The new tug *Ness Point* was delivered at a cost of £7576.10s. 7p
1938	During February severe damage was caused to railway installations by high tides and gale force winds.
1946	Repairs to bomb damage to the station, goods shed, works and offices cost £53,009.
1948	The railways became a nationalised industry with the LNER becoming part of the newly formed British Railways.
1953	During January severe damage was caused to railway installations by high tides and gale force winds. The Breydon Viaduct closed.

1958	In October, the 50 foot high sand and shingle plant on the Old Extension, rebuilt by the LNER in the 1930s closed. Installation of the latest automatic British built sleeper handling equipment commenced at the Sleeper Depot.
1959	The new sleeper handling and production plant was commissioned.
1960	The sand and shingle plant, at one time of great importance, was demolished.
1962	The last active steam locomotive to be based in the Norwich Division, Class J17 65567, was reallocated to March shed at the end of March after working an enthusiast's rail tour. The locomotive had received special attention by Norwich shed staff prior to working the rail tour and had been kept in superb mechanical condition, the work being overseen by the legendary Mr. Bill Harvey.
1963	Responsibility for the harbour and the shipping fleet passed from British Transport Commission - British Railways (Eastern Region) to the British Transport Docks Board. Tug ownership ceased. It was proposed that the East Suffolk railway line between Lowestoft and Ipswich should be closed.
1964	The Sleeper Depot, at one time of national importance, closed.
1966	The Minister of Transport announced that after considering the vast number of representations made against closure, the East Suffolk line would not be closed. Plans were drawn up to extensively modernise and rationalise the line. These were to include automated level crossings, singling of much of the track, withdrawal of the remaining goods facilities, de-staffing the stations, and a modern system of train control based on radio signalling.
1970	On the 2nd May, the 9.10 pm Yarmouth Southtown to Lowestoft Central passenger train became the last train to run over the coast line between the two towns. Thousands of people turned out to witness the sad and to many, short-sighted closure decision.
1971	During January, demolition of the coast railway line between Lowestoft and Yarmouth was nearing completion. The land formerly comprising the trackbed and some stations was used for the building of new roads, retail premises and housing developments. One station on the line was saved from demolition for use as residential purposes.
1972	Closure was announced of the remaining sections of the south side branch line.
1973	Last consignment of fish by-products left Lowestoft by rail on the 27th September.
1982	Port responsibilities passed to Associated British Ports.
1984	The last locomotive hauled through service train ran between Lowestoft and London on the 12th May.
1997	Following the break up of British Rail, the last rail services provided by that organisation from Lowestoft ran in January. Local and intercity passenger services were taken over by Anglia Railways and the infrastructure by Railtrack.
1998	A joint announcement in June by English, Welsh and Scottish (EWS), a rail freight operator, and Railtrack stated that rail freight services would return to Lowestoft after more than a decade. A section of the large good yards would be upgraded to accommodate the trains after lying unused for many years. Despite much initial optimism, the trains were infrequent with gaps of many months between them. EWS locomotives, classes 31, 37, 47, 56, 66 and 67, hauled those that did run.
1999	During January it was announced by Anglia Railways that a daily through service to London from Lowestoft, routed over the restrictive Lowestoft - Ipswich line, would be reintroduced in May after a fifteen-year absence. The trains used would be Class 170 diesel multiple units, stopping at all stations on the line. In subsequent timetables, the through service was reduced to one in each direction and the Sunday service discontinued.
2000	It was announced during March that a company, with a chain of public houses, was interested in developing the facilities at Lowestoft station, not currently in use, as a public house/restaurant.
2002	In January 2002, plans were announced for the much-needed enhancement of services on the two lines serving Lowestoft. These plans quickly brought some dissent from motorists and other road users, who complained that the increased number of trains serving the community would mean use of the level crossings in Oulton Broad, and hence cause greater inconvenience to road traffic. Those interested in improving road traffic flows, again mooted long running suggestions that Lowestoft station should be moved or closed completely, and that the railway lines from Ipswich and Norwich be terminated at Oulton Broad away from the town centre.

EXAMPLES OF STEAM LOCOMOTIVES SEEN AT LOWESTOFT

Top   LNER 3 Cylinder Class K3 2-6-0.Tractive Power at 85% Boiler Pressure 30,031lbs. Tender capacity 4200 gallons and 7.5 tons of coal
Bottom LNER 3 Cylinder Class B17 4-6-0.Tractive Power at 85% Boiler Pressure 25,380lbs. Tender capacity 3700 gallons and 4 tons of coal.
Regrettably, no examples of either a Class B17 or K3 have been preserved.

THE LOWESTOFT - NORWICH LINE

The first station on the line to Norwich is Oulton Broad North, by far one of the busiest local intermediate stations. These photographs show the station in the 1950s, complete with footbridge, waiting rooms and gated level crossing. The footbridge was demolished in January 1974.

At the time of writing, proposals by Anglia Railways, the train operating company, to improve services on the line have been opposed by some road users because of increased delays caused by the more frequent closure of the level crossing.

Left - View from the Up platform looking east.

Right - View from the Up platform looking west.

For a great many years Lowestoft had a fine selection of through trains to many destinations. The service to York was one of these, and always popular. In this scene, recorded at Oulton Broad North and taken from the now demolished footbridge, we witness the arrival of this train headed by a 800hp British Thomson Houston/Clayton Type 1 diesel electric locomotive. Designed for local freight work, these locomotives were introduced in 1957 and equipped with a Paxman engine. In 1984, they became the Class 15 of which one, No. D8233, has been preserved and is based at Crewe.

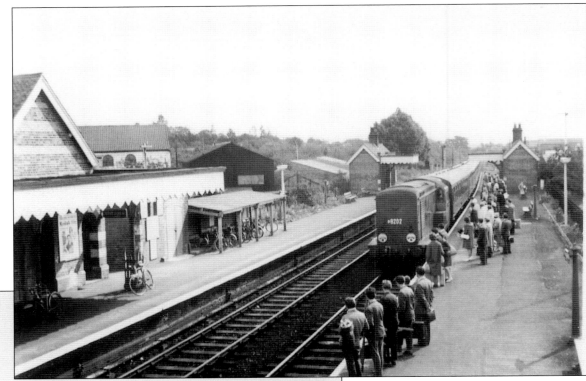

Known to railway enthusiasts as the "Dub Dees", the Riddles designed War Department 2-8-0 heavy freight locomotives, occasionally worked through to Lowestoft. Recorded at Oulton Broad North whilst employed on a special working, No. 90520 is seen at the coal sidings in what is today the doctor's surgery and car park.

A batch of Class J17 0-6-0 goods locomotives were for many years shedded at Lowestoft. In addition to being employed on hauling local goods trains, they were often to be found working passenger trains. This particular locomotive, No. 65586, was allocated to Norwich shed and is seen here being employed on engineering duties at Oulton Broad North. Forerunners of this class, designed by J. Holden, were introduced in 1901. One of this class is preserved and is part of the National Collection based at York.

A type frequently seen on the routes to Lowestoft in the 1950s, the Class B1 4-6-0 was designed by Edward Thompson and introduced in 1942. Here we see one of the class, No. 61043, at Oulton Broad North shunting whilst on goods train duties. Fortunately, two examples of this well known type of locomotive have been preserved.

Class J15 0-6-0 No. 65435 shunting at the Caldecott Road sidings in August 1954. The maltings at Oulton Broad at that time were operational, and connected to the national railway network. These sidings served the cattle pens and also gave rail access to the maltings.

Dieselisation came early to East Anglia with some of the first diesel multiple units arriving in the summer of 1955. One of the early types is seen approaching Oulton Broad from Norwich in the late 1950s.

Visits to Lowestoft by the Class 67 locomotives have become quite frequent with their use on special passenger workings in addition to freight duties. The two day annual air display held in July each year, brings massive crowds to the beach and sea front. Many thousands of spectators use the additional trains and buses laid on by Anglia Railways for the event. The special trains on the Norwich line have been hauled formations, the locomotives used for these being Classes 31, 47 and 67. Here, Class 67 No. 67020, running non-stop from Norwich rattles the buildings as it thunders through Oulton Broad North on the 26th July 2001.

Upon their introduction in 1957, the Brush Type 2 diesel electric A1A- A1A locomotives replaced many classes of steam locomotives including the Thompson B1s and Gresley B17s.

One of this type is seen running light engine through Oulton Broad North in the late 1950s. Under the 1968 renumbering scheme, the early members of the class became Class 30; however, after redesign work had been carried out, all members of the class eventually became Class 31.

Somerleyton Swing Bridge is one of two swing bridges on the route between Lowestoft and Norwich. This particular bridge replaced an earlier one in 1902-03, prior to the line being doubled, and cost £9039 to construct.

Haddiscoe station and the adjacent rail network has an interesting and very complex history. Originally located near the present day large road bridge, it eventually moved to the present location around 1904. Another station, St. Olaves Junction Station, later renamed Herringfleet Junction, existed to the east of the present station. It was basically an interchange for passengers wishing to transfer from Lowestoft to Norwich services to those for Yarmouth. This view of Haddiscoe Station is from a Yarmouth Southtown - London train taken on the last day of services over that line, in November 1959.

Many rail passengers unfamiliar with the section of line running alongside the "New Cut" can be surprised at the closeness and, at times, height of the water. The "New Cut" joins the River Yare at Reedham with the River Waveney at Haddiscoe and was completed in 1833 as part of the plan to link the city of Norwich with the new Lowestoft Harbour. It was for many years a railway responsibility. This 1903 view shows part of the "New Cut" and the location of the first Haddiscoe Station near to the level crossing gates on the left. The vessel passing through the bridge is the *Jeanie Hope*, an iron steam coaster built in 1881.

Standard Class 4MT 2-6-0 No. 76079 heads "The Easterling", a special train, through Somerleyton station on the 4th May 2002. This, the first steam hauled passenger train seen at Lowestoft since 1962, had started at London Liverpool Street and travelled to Lowestoft via Norwich. It returned to London via the East Suffolk Line. The original train of that name was, Sunday excepted, a daily summer service from London to Yarmouth Southtown and Lowestoft, and is featured on the cover of this book. No. 76079 is one of a class of 115 locomotives built between 1952 and 1957 for British Railways. Four have been preserved. This type of locomotive was a development of the Ivatt LMS 4MT, which were frequently seen working Yarmouth Beach trains at Lowestoft. Somerleyton Station opened with the line to Reedham in 1847.

Anglia Railways Class 170 diesel multiple units are daily visitors to Lowestoft. This scene featuring another view of the New Cut, shows No. 170399 between Haddiscoe and Reedham whilst working the 10.45 am Lowestoft to Norwich service on the 8th April 2002.

Another Class 67 diesel locomotive is seen heading an afternoon freight on the 29th May 2001. Having just passed through Haddiscoe, we find No. 67004 heading a train loaded with recycled material for the offshore oil and gas industry. These trains commenced running between Lowestoft and Aberdeen in June 1998. Although a wide variety of motive power has been used on them, the most common have been either Class 66 or 67 locomotives.

The second of the bridges on the route to Norwich, is at Reedham. As with Somerleyton bridge, this replaced an earlier one in 1902-03 prior to doubling of the track. This view is not available to the rail traveller and captures the bridge opened for the motor coaster *Rose Julie M* to pass through. Built in 1941, she was owned by Thomas Metcalf and is probably heading for the port of Norwich with a cargo of coal. Vessels such as this no longer visit the city.

The majority of present day local services in East Anglia are provided by Classes 150 and 153 diesel multiple units, both types are not very popular with passengers who have long legs due to restricted legroom! Complete in the latest Anglia livery, a Class 150 forming a Lowestoft to Norwich service approaches Reedham station in April 2002. The imposing 1904 Reedham Junction Signal Box, which the unit is passing, replaced an earlier box when the Lowestoft line was doubled. The junction of the Yarmouth via Berney Arms, and the Lowestoft routes is to the east of this box.

The present station at Reedham replaced the original, which was fifteen chains to the east of the existing structure, in June 1904. A fast Lowestoft train formed by a Class 170 diesel multiple unit passes through the present station in April 2002.

The down platform is now directly linked by a footpath to a large housing estate built adjacent to the station. The boarded end of the footpath is visible at the end of the canopy on the down platform.

The sugar factory at Cantley adjacent to the Lowestoft to Norwich line first opened in 1912. After closure during the First World War, it reopened in 1920. It was rail connected for many years and the bulk of the materials used at the plant, as well as products from it, were carried by rail.

A complex railway system existed complete with its own green liveried locomotives and rolling stock. In recent years, the plant had two yellow liveried diesel shunters. This is now history, for having decided that rail facilities were no longer required, the sidings were removed and all stock disposed of. This scene, showing one of the diesel shunters, was taken in the early 1990s from a passing Lowestoft train.

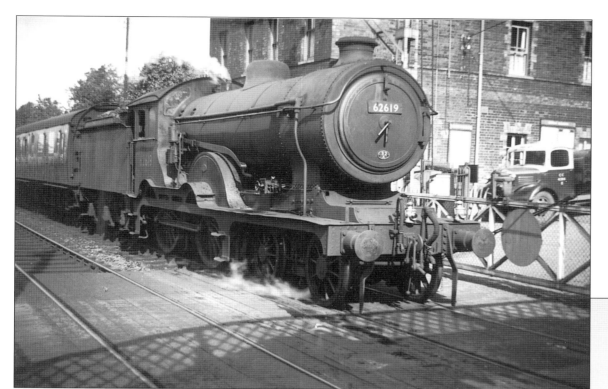

Brundall station presents a pleasant scene on 6th September 1956, with D16/3 4-4-0 No. 62619, complete with original footplating, waiting at the station with a stopping train to the coast. The British Railway lorry parked by the side of the station completes the picture. This locomotive ended her days at Norwich, and was withdrawn from service during September 1957.

Brush Class 31 A1A-A1A No. 31187 is seen running light engine to Norwich slowing for a signal check at Brundall, on the 14th August 1993.

Trains from Norwich to the coastal resorts were often hauled by Class B12/3 4-6-0s. These locomotives were the Gresley rebuild of the original Stephen Holden design introduced in 1911.

One of this fine class, No. 61572, is owned by the Midland and Great Northern Railway Society, having been purchased for preservation in 1961. It is normally to be found on the very scenic North Norfolk Railway, whose headquarters are at Sheringham.

Left - An action shot of the Norwich allocated Class B12/3 No. 61514 as it storms out of the city heading for the coast in February 1957.

Another of the Norwich allocation of B12/3s, a very clean No. 61547 waits to depart from Thorpe station. It was allocated to Norwich for many years leaving there in the autumn of 1958 for storage at Stratford, where it was cut up for scrap in December that year.

Designed at Derby and introduced in 1951, the Britannia Class 7MT 4-6-2 locomotives revolutionised rail service in East Anglia, and in the late 1950s and early 1960s could be seen at Lowestoft.
One of these locomotives, No. 70001 *Lord Hurcomb*, arrives at Norwich. A section of the vast locomotive depot can be seen in the background.

Displaying the Norwich 32A shed plate on the smokebox door, No. 70010 *Owen Glendower* is seen waiting to leave Norwich with a London Liverpool Street train.

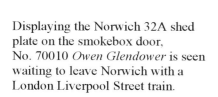

Contrasting with the Britannia's on the previous page, Class J15 No. 65469 was involved in removing empty stock from Platform 5 at Norwich on the 20th February 1957. The locomotive is displaying the headcode appropriate for an express or newspaper train!

A familiar scene to Lowestoft travellers at Norwich, were the Class J50 0-6-0 tank locomotives undertaking station pilot duties. This class, a Gresley Great Northern design, was introduced in 1922, the result of a rebuild of locomotives built just before the First World War. On 20th February 1957, No. 68899 was on duty at the station.

Since the end of regular main line steam traction, numerous appearances have been made by steam locomotives in East Anglia. One example is shown here, another can be found on the following page.

Many locomotives arrived at Norwich for breaking up in the yard of A. King & Sons. Several of these were relatively modern and some in very good condition. Coming directly out of main line service following the end of steam on the Southern Region, Standard Class 4MT 4-6-0s No. 75074, 75075 and 75077 arrived, complete, for cutting up. At the time, the connecting and coupling rods were stored in the tender of No. 75077, the locomotive featured here. These scenes were recorded in November 1967. Locomotives such as these in a complete condition and just out of service would be in great demand today by heritage railways and preservation societies, and would be worth large sums of money. Many trucks, box vans and guards vans are also seen waiting to be cut up. Parts of these locomotives were later exported as scrap through Lowestoft Docks.

In May 1967 the well known Gresley Class A3 4-6-2 60103 *Flying Scotsman,* as LNER No. 4472, led the return to steam traction on the main lines of East Anglia when it brought two charter trains to the city. These were "The East Anglian" on the 6th and the "The Norfolkman" on the 20th.

Top Left - Without the paraphernalia of electrification, No. 4472 with two tenders approaches the city after crossing Trowse Swing Bridge.

Top Right - During the time that No. 4472 was at Norwich station, the public were allowed in the cab.

Bottom Right - With the removal of the train, *Flying Scotsman* reverses to Crown Point to turn on the triangle there. Of interest are the diesel locomotives on shed; these include four Class 31s and one Class 37, and also the sidings in the foreground, full of mixed stock.

A comprehensive view of Beccles Station in the 1950s with Class B17/6 61669 *Barnsley* paused whilst working a stopping train to the coast. Here the train would be divided, with the section of the train destined for Lowestoft being detached and taken on the final leg of the journey by a locomotive waiting on an adjacent line. Many features of this important junction station at that time are to be seen. These include the footbridges, the island platform canopy, and the bay platform. Many parcels are being taken off the train by a member of the station staff.

A number of the Gresley Class K3 2-6-0s were shedded at Lowestoft. Having just joined the East Suffolk line, Gresley Class K3 2-6-0 No. 61939 approaches Gravel Pit level crossing with an express fish train in August 1954.

Britannia Class 7MT 4-6-2 No. 70040 *Clive of India* takes the East Suffolk line at Oulton Broad North Junction with a London express. The large, railway served, Esso fuel distribution depot on the right was set up by the Anglo American Oil Co. in 1920, and is now closed.

The first station on the East Suffolk Line to Ipswich is Oulton Broad South. The well-kept station is seen here in the late 1950s. Many changes took place starting in September 1966, and included the stations becoming unstaffed and removal of much of the double track as part of a modernisation plan. The station is now a Token Exchange Point on the Radio Electronic Token Block between Westerfield Junction, near Ipswich, and Oulton Broad North Junction, controlled from Saxmundham.

The Brush Type 2 diesel electric locomotives were one of the first main line diesel classes to appear in large numbers in East Anglia. One of that type, D5549, is seen taking the East Suffolk Line at Oulton Broad whilst heading a Lowestoft to London through working in the early 1960s. Introduced in 1957; under the 1968 renumbering scheme many members of the class initially became Class 30, however after redesign work had been carried out they all became Class 31.

One of the Lowestoft Gresley Class K3 2-6-0s, No. 61949, leaves Oulton Broad South for Lowestoft with a train from Ipswich in the early 1950s.

One of the first Brush Type 2s to be delivered to the Eastern Region, crosses Oulton Broad Swing Bridge in the 1950s with a through express working from London to Lowestoft. This bridge replaced the earlier one at this location in 1908, and was originally known as Carlton Colville Swing Bridge.

Designed by J. Holden, Class E4 2-4-0 No. 62797 hurries through Oulton Broad South on the 23rd March 1957, whilst returning from shunting work on the East Suffolk line. Built for the GER in 1902, this locomotive was originally Class T26 No. 416.

As increasing numbers of diesel locomotives became available to work the Norwich - London trains in the late 1950s, the displaced Standard Class 7MT 4-6-2 Britannia class locomotives started to appear on the East Suffolk line with workings from London to Lowestoft and also Yarmouth Southtown. Here we see *Britannia* herself approaching Gravel Pit level crossing at Harbour Road in Oulton Broad, having just crossed the Swing Bridge

A snowy scene in early 1959 from the footbridge at Victoria Road level crossing in Oulton Broad, before the crossing gates and bridge were removed, the crossing keepers cottage demolished, and much of the East Suffolk Line was singled. Gresley Class B17/4 4-6-0 61660 *Hull City* approaches with a Lowestoft - London train. *Hull City* was allocated to Lowestoft shed at the time. After a period in store at Stratford, it was broken up there in June 1960.

Many traditional features of the railway scene are no longer to be seen, especially on the East Suffolk Line between Lowestoft and Ipswich. These include the signal box and the siding, seen here at Barnby, between Lowestoft and Beccles.

Following the modernisation of the line and the introduction of radio signalling, signal boxes were made redundant and removed. Sidings were also dismantled or taken out of use following the withdrawal of goods facilities.

Taking your holiday in a railway Camping Coach was very popular for many years. A number were located near Lowestoft at stations such as Lowestoft North, Corton, and Hopton. This one could be found at Oulton Broad South.

Beccles station was an important railway junction, with passenger services to the east, west, north and south of the town. In addition, vast amounts of freight and goods passed through. Back in GER days, the Norwich train can be seen in the bay platform on the left together with a well stocked bookstall and milk churns under the footbridge. Plans are presently (2002) being drawn up to enhance the area around the station. The large rail connected maltings adjacent to the station have been demolished, and replaced by housing.

Looking across from the substantial island platform at Beccles in August 1953, we find J. Holden designed Class J17 0-6-0 No. 65507, in the sidings with a local goods train.
It was allocated to Lowestoft shed and is here running with a small tender. No. 65507 was transferred away from Lowestoft during December 1958, after many years at the shed.

A superb scene on Whit Monday 1957, as two Gresley 4-6-0s prepare to depart from a very busy Beccles station. Class B17/6 No. 61664 *Liverpool* and Class B17/1 No. 61602 *Walsingham* are heading a combined Lowestoft and Yarmouth train to London Liverpool Street. Both No. 61602 and No. 61664 were allocated to Yarmouth Southtown shed for many years. No. 61602 was scrapped in March 1958 at Doncaster and No. 61664 scrapped at Stratford in June 1960.

The Cravens Class 105 two car diesel multiple units (DMUs), were at one time a familiar sight in East Anglia. One of the class is seen crossing Beccles Swing Bridge on the Yarmouth - Beccles line, which closed in November 1959. Locally most of these units were replaced by Metropolitan Cammell Class 101 DMUs. These were to become the last type of the early generation of DMUs to be used on Lowestoft services.

It is the 2nd November 1959, and the final day of services on the Beccles - Yarmouth line. Class B1 4-6-0 No. 61051 arrives at Beccles with one of the last Yarmouth to London through trains to travel over the line. After closure of the line, these trains were routed via Lowestoft. However, in 1962 Vauxhall station took over responsibility for the London services at Yarmouth, these then being routed via Norwich. On summer Saturdays until September 1966, up to nine London through services still used Yarmouth Southtown, these running via the East Suffolk line, reversing at Lowestoft and then via the coast line. All stopped at Gorleston, and some at Hopton and Corton.

Classes F6 2-4-2T No. 67231 and F5 2-4-2T No. 67216 leave Beccles in the mid 1950s with the through Lowestoft carriages off a train from Liverpool Street. No. 67231 appears to be doing all the work, and it is possible that No. 67216 has failed. At one time Lowestoft shed was allocated many 2-4-2 tank locomotives, and by March 1958, all had been withdrawn.

On a very overcast cold day at Beccles in the early 1950s, the Lowestoft coaches are collected from Platform 4 by Gresley B17/6 4-6-0 No. 61665 *Leicester City* for attaching to the front of a London bound train. The Yarmouth coaches forming the other part of this train are visible on the left. On arrival in London, Lowestoft passengers did not have to walk so far as those from Yarmouth! The moveable section of Platform 3, not an original feature of Beccles Station, can be seen. This could be swung across the line to form a bridge and thus give level access between the island and main platforms. A porter has collected parcels from the train and has also removed the tail lamp from the last coach.

This typical East Suffolk line local goods train was recorded at Beccles on the 2nd March 1957 with Class B12/3 4-6-0 No. 61564 in charge. These locomotives were originally designed by S. D. Holden for express passenger duties, being introduced in 1911. Later the majority of the class was rebuilt by Gresley. No. 61564 was allocated to Ipswich shed remaining there until November 1958, when it was withdrawn for breaking up. As mentioned elsewhere, thankfully one of these impressive machines was purchased for preservation by the M&GN Railway Society and can usually be found at home on the North Norfolk Railway at Sheringham.

Another fine example of a Class B12/3, No. 61535 arrives with safety valves open at Beccles after a fast run from Ipswich, with an express from London Liverpool Street to Yarmouth and Lowestoft. The 3rd of March 1957, when this dramatic scene was recorded, was cold and overcast with drizzle. To see these superb locomotives working schedules alongside the modern Britannia locomotives was a lasting tribute to the original Holden design, the Gresley rebuild, and the staff that maintained them. No. 61535 was well known for the highly polished metal work and cream painted cab. It was scrapped at Stratford in January 1960.

Brampton station and signal box present an idyllic railway scene in this early 1960s view.
Today it is totally different. The main station buildings on the up platform were demolished in April 1978, and the former Midland & Great Northern shelter on the down platform was removed and is now preserved at a railway heritage site in Essex. Brampton is 104 miles 49 chains from London Liverpool Street, on the single line section between Beccles and Halesworth.

The Crossing, Halesworth.

Originally, there was a level crossing at Halesworth station where the A144 Norwich road crossed the railway. This required a section of each platform to be movable, and to swing across the line to allow road traffic to pass. Although not operational now, these sections were cosmetically restored in 1999. This interesting scene, from the 1920s, shows the level crossing closed for a train to pass and road traffic held up. The problem of road traffic being disrupted at this level crossing led to a bridge being built, after a successful campaign by the local council.

Perhaps the most unusual feature of the Lowestoft - Ipswich line was the Halesworth station of the narrow gauge Southwold Railway (SR). This was situated adjacent to the main line station. A train from Southwold is seen arriving at the SR Halesworth station headed by one of the two original Sharp, Stewart 2-4-0 tank locomotives. The gauge of the SR, which opened in 1879 and closed in 1929, was 3ft. and the length, excluding the branch lines, was 8 miles 63 chains. In total, the SR owned four steam locomotives. Recently there has been an initiative to reopen part of this fascinating line. However, these plans have met with strong opposition from some local residents.

S.8003.   HALESWORTH STATION, SOUTHWOLD RAILWAY

G.E. RAILWAY STATION, HALESWORTH.

Above - The Halesworth to Beccles part of the Lowestoft - Ipswich line was the first part opened by the East Suffolk Railway on the 4th December 1854. Halesworth station is 100 miles 53 chains from Liverpool Street, and at the end of the long single line section from Oulton Broad North Junction. Seen here in GER days, the buildings on the up platform have now all been demolished but those on the down platform are intact. This building has a number of uses, one part forming the town's museum.

Right - For many years a large rail served dairy existed at Halesworth, which somewhat overshadowed the station. With a large number of sidings at the station, a daily need existed for a locomotive to carry out shunting and yard duties there. This duty was assigned to a Lowestoft locomotive, such as a Class E4 or J15, both designed by J. Holden for the GER. A Lowestoft locomotive for over ten years, Class J15 0-6-0 No. 65462 is seen at Halesworth with the dairy in the background. This area now consists of roads and a housing estate. No. 65462 is displaying a light engine headcode ready for the journey back home to Lowestoft. In June 1960 it was transferred away from Lowestoft. This locomotive survives in the twenty-first century at the North Norfolk Railway.

Top Left - A very sad day at Saxmundham on the 10th September 1966. As Stratford based Brush Type 4 (Class 47) Co-Co No. D1780 leaves Saxmundham with a London Liverpool Street-Lowestoft train, the last but one train from Aldeburgh arrives. For the last day this was formed by two Metropolitan-Cammell Class 101 diesel multiple units. These made one more return trip up the branch bringing an end to rail services to Aldeburgh.

Bottom Far Left - Leiston as seen from the last train down the line. The branch still exists through this station, to serve Sizewell Power Station.

Bottom Left - The front of the leading diesel multiple unit of the final train to Aldeburgh, with the indicator showing for the last time, that the train was destined for Aldeburgh.

Taken from a glass plate negative, the Saxmundham - Aldeburgh train is seen progressing along the branch in GER days.

The locomotive on this service is typically a GER Class Y14 0-6-0, later to become Class J15. The usual motive power on the branch consisted of GER types such as a 2-4-2 tank locomotive or a J15. However an Ivatt 2MT 2-6-2 tank locomotive was at one time used.

Another print taken from a glass plate negative from GER days, showing a J. Holden designed Class F3 2-4-2 tank locomotive, with a a train for Aldeburgh at Saxmundham. With advertised connecting services, it is waiting for the the Liverpool Street to Lowestoft and Yarmouth train to arrive with possible passengers for Leiston, Thorpeness and Aldeburgh.

Only a short time after the class was introduced in 1911, a Holden GER Class S46 4-6-0, later to become the Class B12, leaves Saxmundham with a London Liverpool Street to Lowestoft train.

The short down platform now in use at Saxmundham has a certain "temporary" look about it. This is opposite the up platform and replaced the original on the down side which was staggered from the up platform.

Wickham Market station is located 84 miles 42 chains from London Liverpool Street and is situated on the East Suffolk Line between Saxmundham and Melton stations. The Framlingham and the Snape branches left the East Suffolk line to the north of this station. Much has changed since this scene was recorded in the early 1960s, when the well kept and tidy station was complete with sidings, loading bay, signal box, and numerous other features which went to make up the complete rural railway station.

Ipswich in steam days saw a wide variety of locomotives types. At the end of the East Suffolk line from Lowestoft, it is 68 miles 59 chains from Liverpool Street. In the latter days of steam much attention was given to the Class 7MT 4-6-2 Britannias. However, a cross section of different types is featured on these pages. A number of Class J15 0-6-0s were fitted with side window cabs for working the Colne Valley line. One of these, No. 65391, has just arrived at Ipswich after working a stopping train from Cambridge on the 30th July 1957.

Class B12 4-6-0 locomotives have been a familiar sight at Ipswich ever since they were introduced on the GER in 1911. No. 61555 arrives with a train from Bury St. Edmunds on the 31st July 1957. Perhaps one day a scene such this will be repeated with No. 61572 from the North Norfolk Railway.

The other end of the station, as usual, was busy. Thompson Class B1 4-6-0 No. 61004 *Oryx* suddenly bursts out of the tunnel with the 1.45 pm train to Peterborough. The date is the 31st July 1957.

LMS Ivatt 2MT 2-6-0 No. 46466 waits to depart from Ipswich in July 1954 with the author, then a young trainspotter, posing on the platform. Introduced in 1946 and designed by H. G. Ivatt, this class was very versatile and saw service in different regions, replacing many older time expired types of small locomotives.

The Ivatt 2MT formed the basis for the British Railway Standard Class 2MT, which was introduced in 1953. No. 46466 was one of a trio allocated to Cambridge shed at the time.

Three light engines proceed through the tunnel, to go to the sheds on the 1st August 1957. They are, from left to right, Class 2MT 2-6-0 No. 46469, Class J17 0-6-0 No. 65578, and Class L1 2-6-4 No. 67706.

A regular performer on the East Suffolk line hauling the London trains serving Lowestoft and Yarmouth, Class B17/6 4-6-0 No.61665 *Leicester City,* waits while the fireman tops up the tender with water before entering Ipswich Tunnel en route to London Liverpool Street. The date is the 3rd August 1957.

THE LOWESTOFT-YARMOUTH LINE

A fine view of a Brush Type 2 locomotive, later designated Class 31, hauling a London -Yarmouth Southtown through train between Lowestoft Central and North stations. This section of line, the majority of which was in a cutting, consisted of a continuous climb with sweeping bends. The date is the 24th July 1966. Today the area is filled with housing, and the track bed has become a cycle way and footpath. All but two of the many bridges on this section remain.

One of the last two Class F6 2-4-2 tank locomotives at Lowestoft, 67229, is seen working a Yarmouth to Lowestoft afternoon train in March 1957 approaching Laundry Lane crossing. This was adjacent to the Eastern Coach Works factory and is now part of the North Quay Retail Park.

Holden designed Class J17 0-6-0 No. 65558 approaches Lowestoft North with one of the summer Saturday London to Gorleston-on-Sea through trains, the "Holiday Camps Express", in the 1950s. It is in the cutting at the back of Worthing Road. Such was the popularity of the holiday camps at Corton, Hopton and Gorleston that four of these express trains ran in the early 1950s between Liverpool Street and Gorleston. The fastest journey time was 3hrs 2mins, the London to Lowestoft part of the journey being covered in 2hrs 33mins No. 65558 was withdrawn from service in January 1960.

Another view of the cutting behind Worthing Road with Class J15 0-6-0 No. 65472 working hard on the climb from Central station with a stopping train for Yarmouth. It is the afternoon of the 12th April 1957.

Lowestoft North station was a popular destination for the military authorities moving large numbers of personnel to camps and establishments near to that station such as on the North Denes, or to what is now Corton Road playing field. Just before the First World War the 4th Battalion Suffolk Regiment is seen marching to their camp having just left the train. This would have reversed at Lowestoft Central and then proceeded to the North station. An interesting feature of this scene is the tram track, which at that time went as far as the town boundary.

The only GNR designed locomotives to be seen on a daily basis at Lowestoft were the H. A. Ivatt designed Class C12 4-4-2 tank locomotives, which were introduced in 1898. No. 67366 of that class is seen here propelling a Yarmouth bound train into Lowestoft North station on 29th July 1957

Featured on this page are two locomotives with over sixty years difference in their designs, both at work on the Lowestoft to Yarmouth line.

T. Worsdell designed Class J15 0-6-0 No. 65478 approaches Hubbards Loke crossing between Corton and Lowestoft North stations, with a Lowestoft train. The field, with Corton Road beyond, is now used for sports activities.

Ivatt Class 4MT 2-6-0 locomotives were for many years the most common type of locomotive found on the former M&GN lines. One of the class, No. 43161 is busy shunting at Lowestoft North, an area now given over to housing, where the author lives. For many years No. 43161 was shedded at Yarmouth Beach and was one of the last locomotives to leave the shed in February 1959, upon closure of the former M&GN main line running from Yarmouth Beach direct to the Midlands.

One station on the line between Lowestoft and Yarmouth still exists, that at Corton, now in use as a private residence. Posing for the camera in 1904, we find a gang of railway navvies working on the platform at that station.

This view of Corton in the early 1960s, is from the down platform and looking towards Lowestoft North. Along with others on the line, the station became unstaffed in September 1966 and closed on the 2nd May 1970. For many years this station was home to two camping coaches.

Left - Except for Gorleston Links Halt, the station at Hopton-on-Sea was typical of the intermediate stations on the line, opening on the 13th July 1903. It is seen here in the late 1950s. As at Corton, two camping coaches were stationed here for many years. One of the Pullman Camping Coaches can be seen on the extreme left of this photograph. It was customary to stable coaches forming one of the "Holiday Camps Express" sets, here or at Gorleston, when not required.

Below - An everyday scene at Hopton in the 1950s. On the 9th September 1957, Class D16/3 4-4-0 No 62570 leaves whilst working a stopping train between Yarmouth Southtown and Lowestoft Central. No. 62570 was allocated to Yarmouth Southtown shed for many years. No trace exists of this station and the yard today, the area having become a large housing estate. On summer Saturdays, hundreds of holiday makers would arrive at Hopton for their annual holidays at the many holiday camps and centres in the village.

The bleak platforms at Gorleston Links Halt are well illustrated in this scene recorded on 9th September 1957. No. 62570 is returning to Yarmouth Southtown having completed the service mentioned on the previous page

Gorleston Links Halt was situated on a high and exposed embankment with no shelter for the passengers on the concrete platforms. Here we find Class J39/1 0-6-0 No. 64731 pounding through the station with a track relaying train.

The Lowestoft - Yarmouth line was being upgraded to main line standards at the time. This view, looking towards Hopton was recorded on the 21st June 1959, one month before this locomotive was withdrawn from service. Like so much of this line, no trace can be found of this station, the area now forming a housing development.

The Class J39 was designed by Gresley and introduced in 1926. Prior to withdrawal, No. 64731 was allocated to Norwich.

The largest and most important intermediate station on the line was Gorleston-on-Sea. This very early photograph shows the station shortly after opening with a Holden 0-6-0 tank locomotive heading the Lowestoft train. This is now the site of a roundabout on the dual carriageway Gorleston by pass, which is built on the track bed of the line to Yarmouth. Gorleston station had a large goods yard and shed, several sidings, a taxi rank and a separate booking hall.

Many services on the line between Lowestoft and Yarmouth were worked by push-pull fitted GER or GNR designed tank locomotives. This is a view from one such train as it approaches Gorleston-on-Sea in 1955. The stock of a "Holiday Camps Express" is stabled in a siding on the left. Gorleston-on-Sea station covered a large area with full facilities.

Until 1953, there were two routes from Gorleston into Yarmouth that trains from Lowestoft could take. One of these went to Yarmouth Beach, the former Midland and Great Northern (M&GN) station, and the other went to Southtown station. The line divided at Gorleston North Junction. This view shows the Lowestoft line on the approach to Yarmouth Beach station at the Nelson Road level crossing. The line north to the Midlands is visible in the background.

In order that Lowestoft trains could gain access to the Beach station at Yarmouth, an expensive scheme involving three large engineering projects was devised. These were for a substantial viaduct over Breydon Water, and two other smaller structures for crossing the River Bure, and the road and railway at Vauxhall station. Part of the massive Breydon Viaduct is seen here from a pleasure boat around 1950. Almost £160,000 was spent on just over two miles of track. Services over the viaduct ceased in 1953. Coaching stock stabled at Vauxhall station can be seen at the top left corner under the spans of the viaduct.

Class J17 0-6-0 No. 65581 complete with a tablet catching device on the tender, for working over the single track M&GN system, is seen here at Yarmouth Beach station.
Designed for heavy freight work, it was not unusual to see J17s working passenger trains, especially on the M&GN, and the Joint Railways Committee line between Lowestoft and Yarmouth. Duties included working the heavy through trains from Lowestoft to the Midlands via the M&GN, and also the "Holiday Camps Express" between Lowestoft and Gorleston.

Yarmouth Beach station was well situated for the beach, the sea front and town centre. It was popular with local railway enthusiasts since it was the only local station where Midland Region locomotives could be seen. Complete closure came on the 28th February 1959. These photographs show the station area the day after closure. Prior to closure of the Breydon Viaduct, Lowestoft enjoyed direct services to the Midlands via Yarmouth Beach.

Left - The large signal box

Right - A view looking towards the station with the locomotive shed on the left. A diesel shunter remained to be used in the demolition work.

It is a warm summer afternoon in the mid 1950s and class F6 2-4-2 No. 67229 is waiting at Yarmouth Southtown to take the next train to Lowestoft. In March 1958 the last of the many 2-4-2 tank locomotives allocated to Lowestoft shed were withdrawn for scrapping. These were 67229 and 67231, both of which had been Lowestoft locomotives for many years

The majority of locomotives seen at Yarmouth Beach were Midland types, but a few Eastern Region classes were represented including B12/3 4-6-0s, D16/3 4-4-0s, J17 0-6-0s, and J65 0-6-0Ts.

On the 7th January 1957, Class D16/3 No. 62517 is seen at Yarmouth Beach having just arrived with a train, and is preparing to go to the sheds.

No. 62517 was one of the locomotives which worked from Beach shed just before closure in February 1959.

A truly marvellous scene inside Yarmouth Southtown station in the 19th century, well before the opening of the direct line in 1903. A train, possibly to Lowestoft, headed by an early 2-4-0 locomotive is being prepared to depart. The first services between the two towns started in 1847 via the new Reedham curve to Yarmouth Vauxhall. Another service to Yarmouth commenced in 1872, after the Marsh Junction - St. Olaves Junction spur opened on the 1st June that year. This spur was located east of the present Haddiscoe station and much of the track bed is still visible today. The trains then ran via the East Suffolk Railway to Southtown.

Once a substantial main line station with all facilities, Yarmouth Southtown
rapidly became a shadow of its former self, after the London through trains
were diverted to the town's Vauxhall station. These scenes were recorded
in April 1975, by which time the main building had become badly run down.

Above - No longer required for railway use, the building was used by a
company involved in the offshore oil and gas industry.
Right - The area previously occupied by the station building, trackbed and
platforms, now form part of a dual carriageway road. At the time this scene
was recorded, industrial premises had already been built on some of the
former trackbed.

TRAVELLING TIMES WITH THE LONDON AND NORTH EASTERN RAILWAY
by
Peter Killby

My parents both originally came from London, which was where our nearest relatives lived. In the early 1930s, times were hard, and my memories of this period are of very occasional trips on a Sunday excursion train leaving Lowestoft about 10.00 am and arriving back about midnight. Family holidays were spent at home and I remember being thrilled in the summer of 1933 at being invited to spend a fortnight with my Grandparents in London. Since there was a through service to Liverpool Street about 8.30 am, I was allowed to travel on my own which horrified my Grandmother when she met me at the other end. At the conclusion of the holiday, on reaching Liverpool Street to my great disgust I was put in the Guard's care and travelled for much of the way in his van. Even at that stage train journey times made a deep impression, for I recollect leaving London at 3.15 pm and reaching Lowestoft at 6.00 pm.

From about 1934 until 1939 we ceased to use the Sunday excursions, and our annual London trip became a much more exciting event at least for my sister and myself. It involved being awoken at around 3.00 am on a Saturday morning, to catch a FA Cup Final excursion to London about an hour later. This train reached London soon after 7.00 am and allowed a very full day in the City. The return service departed from Liverpool Street at midnight and arrived back in Lowestoft about 3.30 am.

I also enjoyed the occasional trips to Yarmouth and these were usually made from Lowestoft North as the fare was cheaper! The route allowed some element of choice, as Yarmouth Southtown was the more convenient destination if visiting the harbour or town centre whilst Yarmouth Beach was very near to Wellesley Road, the home of Great Yarmouth Football Club. The Beach Station was fascinating in that, in addition to departures for the Midlands, there were during the peak summer months small local trains which went only to Potter Heigham but served en route halts such as Scratby and California, which were small wooden structures at ground level. Tickets from these halts were issued by the guard who also produced steps for the passengers boarding or alighting. During the war years, most of my trips were taken by bus as the train service became reduced to about six trains a day in each direction, due to one line being occupied by trucks which stretched most of the way from Lowestoft North to Gorleston.

Following the outbreak of war excursions ceased and my next train journey was of a vastly different nature. Sunday 2nd June 1940 saw the evacuation of all Lowestoft Schools. The destination for the Secondary School at which I was a pupil was Worksop. Our train departed at 11.15 am and was routed via Thetford, March, Spalding, Lincoln and Retford. I had never travelled west of Norwich by rail and this factor made the six-hour journey a pleasant one despite the circumstances. It was more than four years later before the school returned and few of the pupils who left Lowestoft in 1940 remained to make the return journey.

In October 1942 I started work at Norwich and travelled daily from Lowestoft. As clocks were not put back to Greenwich Mean Time during the winter months it was soon a case of doing both journeys under blackout conditions. All carriage windows were fitted with blinds, which remained down and lighting in the compartments was dimmed to such an extent that it was not always possible to read. Carriage heating was provided by steam pipes and was often a topic of interest in that sometimes it would fail to operate, and on other occasions there would prove to be a leakage which would fill a compartment with steam. Several trains bound for Norwich linked up with carriages from Yarmouth at Reedham and with wartime delays it was by no means unusual for the carriages from Lowestoft to be in Reedham sidings for 20 minutes or longer pending the arrival of those from Yarmouth. Even on reaching Norwich there was sometimes the problem of there not being sufficient space for all the carriages to reach the platform, resulting in passengers having to jump down on to the track. Delays were even more pronounced on the 5.12 pm and 5.58 pm return services and I recollect on three occasions, in one week in January 1943, standing on platform one at Norwich until 7.00 pm awaiting the arrival of the train which should have departed for Lowestoft at 5.58 pm. This situation was not helped by the complete absence of any guidance to passengers as to what was happening.

In April 1944 I was called up for service as a Bevin Boy and had to report for coal mining training at Annfield Plain in County Durham. I was pleased to discover the final stage of the journey, from York to Newcastle, would be on the "Flying Scotsman". Sadly, it failed to live up to its title for the 80-mile non-stop journey took a little over 2 hours.

The "Flying Scotsman " in LNER days hauled by a Gresley Class A3 4-6-2.

After initial training I was sent to Shirebrook Colliery in the East Midlands coalfield which was much nearer home. During a twelve month stay at Shirebrook I made several trips home. The journey, which could be made following the day shift, was comparatively quick and involved reaching Worksop for a 4.00 pm departure, followed by changes at Lincoln and March, from whence there was a through service which reached Lowestoft just before midnight. I delayed the return journeys until the last train to Norwich, which on weekdays was 8.40 pm, and 9.10 pm on Sundays, because the mail train from Norwich then had provision for conveying passengers. Changing at Haughley Junction off the 11.35 pm train to London was memorable only because in my experience there was never any sort of lighting in the waiting room. However, I have good memories of March where the staff were particularly kind even to the extent of my being taken to the Supervisors Office, and told to ensure his coal fire was given proper attention. My most memorable journey from Shirebrook though was on VE Day in 1945. I had been partially buried under a roof fall, which resulted in my being put on the Club for a week, which I decided to spend at home. I left Shirebrook at 7.25 am and eventually reached Lowestoft at 6.05 pm. This journey involved seven changes at places such as Lincoln, Boston, Spalding, Kings Lynn and Ely, with stops at more than fifty stations, but it provided an excellent opportunity to see how Eastern England was celebrating the great day. A few months later I was deemed unfit for further service in the mines and call up for military service soon followed. My first posting, after the initial six weeks training, was to the London area so it was often possible to spend weekend leave at home. The first occasion just before Christmas 1945, started rather disastrously as the 12.30 pm fast train to Yarmouth and Lowestoft experienced great difficulty in completing the long climb to Shenfield and eventually took five hours to reach Lowestoft, two hours longer than scheduled. Subsequent trips were considerably better but the service was always at least fifteen minutes late. More than once I missed this train and caught it at Ipswich courtesy of the 12.33 pm service to Norwich, which was non-stop to Ipswich where it was booked to arrive one minute before the Lowestoft train departed.

One memory of the period is of a family, bound for Clacton, discovering they were on the wrong train and taking advantage of a signal stop at Bow Junction, jumping down on the track complete with luggage. We were left to contemplate what problems this must have caused on a very busy stretch of line. To return for Monday morning duty it was feasible to leave Lowestoft at 9.10 pm and, travelling via Norwich, to arrive in London at 4.00 am. In the summer of 1946 I was posted to HQ Southern Command but, despite the extra distance, I still travelled home reasonably often. There was also an occasional Friday evening finish, which enabled me to catch the 10.25 pm mail train to Norwich; this had a 3.20 am connection to Lowestoft. My train back on a Sunday evening was the 6.10 pm through service to Liverpool Street, but in the severe winter of 1946-47 it fell victim to the national coal shortage and it was then a case of changing into a four coach Yarmouth to Ipswich train at Beccles, which was linked to the Norwich to London train at Ipswich. Four coaches were totally inadequate for the numbers travelling, but this situation went on for many weeks until our local Member of Parliament, Mr. Edward Evans, experienced the situation at first hand and made representations in the right quarter.

The "Holiday Camps Express"
leaves Lowestoft hauled by
Gresley K3 2-6-0 No. 61957.

In the long hot summer, which followed, I benefited from the introduction of the 2.45 pm Holiday Camps Express from Liverpool Street to Gorleston, which was booked to run non-stop to Lowestoft in two hours forty minutes. To my disappointment this was never achieved when I travelled, for it was delayed either by a late running slow train to Ipswich or alternatively a failure to pick up sufficient water from the troughs outside Ipswich, which necessitated a stop later on to replenish the supply. In the late autumn, it was my turn to be demobbed and I arrived at Liverpool Street just in time to catch the last direct train of the day to Lowestoft at 5.06 pm, a slow service taking four and a half hours. As I did, I reflected that this was to be my last journey on the London and North Eastern Railway, for on January 1st 1948, British Railways would come into being.

For many years numerous 2-4-2 tank locomotives designed for the Great Eastern Railway hauled the majority of the passenger trains serving Lowestoft. One of these was Class F6 2-4-2T No. 67231 seen here at the Central station. Allocated to Lowestoft shed for many years, it finally left in March 1958 for breaking up. The Class F6 was introduced in 1911, being a development of the Class F4 locomotive.

A scene from 1901 at Lowestoft station showing GER 2-4-0 No. 34 at the buffer stops. No. 34 was built in 1869 by Sharp Stewart. A section of the station roof is visible which, despite much local opposition, was removed in 1992.

An 1895 view of Lowestoft Station showing the main entrance in Denmark Road. This station was completed by Lucas Bros. in 1855 and replaced the earlier one built for the opening of the Lowestoft to Reedham line in 1847. Unfortunately, over the years, this building has been subjected to many alterations and some rebuilding resulting in several of the distinct features it once had being destroyed.

A view inside Lowestoft Central station on the 19th May 1904, with some of the group of ninety people who travelled from the town to Switzerland for a holiday. This visit was organised by Canon Tupper-Carey, who can be seen in the centre of the photograph to the left of the gentleman with a white beard. The group travelled via London Bridge, Dieppe and Paris. Many interesting aspects of the station at that time can be seen in this photograph

In July 1904 the GER set up a bus service between Lowestoft and Southwold using Milnes-Daimler vehicles. Here we see a bus about to depart on the Southwold service from Lowestoft. Other bus services set up by the GER at that time included a circular route to Oulton Broad.

The autumn herring season was a very busy period for the east coast ports of Lowestoft and Yarmouth and their railways. In addition to transporting fish, the railway carried goods associated with the fishery and large numbers of Scottish workers who arrived by special trains. Several of these trains arrived via the Joint Committee line from Yarmouth having travelled to East Anglia via the Midland & Great Northern Railway. Many left the trains at Yarmouth Beach to work there for the season. A few of the hundreds of Scottish fisher girls are seen here at Lowestoft about to board a special Aberdeen train in the 1920s

Hauled by one of James Holden's handsome "Claud Hamilton" 4-4-0 locomotives, a Lowestoft - London express makes an impressive departure from the town. This class of locomotive was designated D56 by the GER and the locomotive seen here was built in 1908. Trains such as this, most of which included restaurant cars, were scheduled to make the journey non-stop in around two and a half hours.

A London to Lowestoft express crosses Oulton Broad Swing Bridge hauled by another of Holden's "Claud Hamilton" locomotives. Before the introduction of the GER Class S46 4-6-0 locomotives in 1911, the small "Claud Hamilton" locomotives achieved remarkable feats in hauling heavy passenger trains over the GER network to very tight running schedules. Perhaps their most pressing task was hauling the "Norfolk Coast Express" non-stop from London Liverpool Street to North Walsham. This train could load to well over 420 tons at weekends, and still reach Cromer from London in 2hrs 55mins.

For a few years during the 1930s, steam driven railcars were used on passenger services at Lowestoft. The type used was built by the Clayton Wagon Co. Ltd., and one is seen here, believed to be 43305 *Transit*, leaving Lowestoft and passing the locomotive sheds. They were not considered an overall success and the services worked by them reverted to conventional carriages hauled by locomotives. A similar unit was construction by the Sentinel Wagon Co. Ltd., but again met with limited success.

Shortly after delivery in 1928, LNER Class B17/1 4-6-0 No. 2801 *Holkham* makes a superb sight on the turntable at Lowestoft. The second of the "Sandringham" Class locomotives to enter service, it was built by the North British Locomotive Company under Works No. 23804 and named after the Earl of Leicester's seat near Wells-next-the-Sea in North Norfolk. In 1948, under the renumbering scheme it became No. 61601 and in January 1958 was withdrawn from service and broken up at Doncaster the following March. Unlike the great majority of the Class B17s, *Holkham* was not rebuilt during its life and retained the Great Eastern pattern 3,500 gallon tender.

One of the large number of Lowestoft allocated GER 2-4-2 tank locomotives, No. 8047, completed in 1902, is seen arriving at Lowestoft with a Yarmouth train in the late 1930s. Originally this locomotive was GER Class C32 No. 1047 and in 1924, under LNER ownership, became Class F3 No. 8047. It was withdrawn in 1947 but was allocated No. 67148 in the 1948 renumbering scheme.

A small number of 4-4-2T locomotives, designed by H. A. Ivatt for the Great Northern Railway, worked for many years from Lowestoft shed. Introduced in 1898 these locomotives became the LNER Class C12. One of the class, LNER No. 4502, is seen here in the late 1930s at Lowestoft Central. In later years they could often be found working services between Lowestoft and Yarmouth, often in the push-pull mode. Locomotives of this class were more powerful than the GER 2-4-2 tank locomotives generally seen on local services at Lowestoft. The large water crane together with coal and water on the ground, give a superb steam atmosphere to this delightful scene.

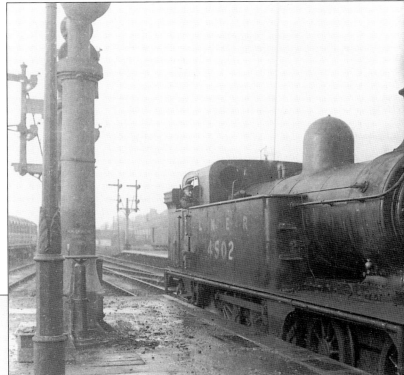

The Second World War brought many changes to Lowestoft. Being on the front line the town and the important railway network, became a prime target for the enemy. Unfortunately this aspect of the town at war has tended to be overlooked in recent times. Several railway installations were repeatedly attacked and badly damaged, with serious loss of life. The LNER Harbour Works, one of three important railway civil engineering facilities in the town, is seen here after a raid in 1941, having received several direct hits with heavy loss of life.

Determined that Hitler would not smash the vital local railway links and infrastructure, the railway staff soon got on the with job of clearing up and restoring that which the enemy had set out to destroy. Just visible is one of the LNER steam cranes which has been moved into position to assist in making the buildings safe. At the present time (2002), the area previously occupied by the historic Harbour Works has been cleared, with rumours that a supermarket is to be built there.

During the Second World War a need existed for rugged, tough, heavy freight locomotives. As a result of this, a new British type, the War Department "Austerity" locomotive was introduced in 1943. There were two versions, a 2-8-0 and a 2-10-0. These were designed under the direction of R. A. Riddles when he was Deputy Director of Royal Engineer Equipment. Visits during the war period were made by the smaller 2-8-0 locomotives to Lowestoft, one of which, No. 70831, is seen here. After the war many hundreds of these were purchased from the Ministry of Supply by the new British Railways for general heavy goods work.

Further scenes of damage caused to railway premises in the town by enemy action during the Second World War at Lowestoft.

An example of the railway helping to fight back. With the need to safeguard Britain's shipping lanes from mines during the war a large number of minesweepers were built, many at Lowestoft and Oulton Broad. In this very rare archive photograph, we see a new motor minesweeper at the North Quay in Lowestoft in the process of having her main engine lowered into place by the LNER Norwich District railway breakdown crane. Many totally underestimate the valuable work carried out by the railway industry locally in times of war. No other facilities existed at the time to carry out this vital task. The crane was normally kept at Norwich, in steam, ready to deal with emergency and high priority tasks such as this.

An every day scene during the mid 1950s only a few yards from the swing bridge in the centre of Lowestoft. Sentinel Class Y3 0-4-0 Departmental Locomotive No. 38 is seen at the western end of the Trawl Dock, having just crossed the A12 trunk road after emerging from the Harbour Works. This comprehensive local railway scene is just one of many recorded by the late Dr. Ian C. Allen, of which a number are in this book. This particular study is full of nostalgia for many local residents. The shops and bank seen in the background have changed owners many times since this photograph was taken, but all still exist in 2002, unlike the Harbour Works.

In 1992 alterations were carried out to parts of Lowestoft Station, the result being that the structure was modernised and simplified. Amongst the work carried out was the total removal of the roof covering the concourse and an area of the platforms. Some brickwork was removed, an area of the platforms was refurbished, a new open, paved concourse created, a few trees were planted and interior alterations carried out to the booking hall and office. One new toilet was provided for the use of all passengers, the previous toilets having been disused for sometime, were demolished as was the once very popular bookstall.
In previous years, the station was renowned for the highly polished copper lamp tops on the platform buffer stops together with the burnished buffers.

Above and Left - Two 1987 views of the interior of the station, with Metropolitan Cammell Class 101 diesel multiple units in platforms two and four. The unit in platform four (on the left), is radio fitted for working the Radio Electronic Token Block signalling system on the East Suffolk line to Ipswich. The area formerly occupied by platform one is now part of the extensive station car park. One feature of the present station much missed by animal lovers is the small drinking bowl provided in the past by railway authorities. The bowl is visible in the bottom left corner of the above photograph.

Lowestoft could boast having by far the most easterly railway lines and sidings in Great Britain. One aspect of the unique railway network in the town was the sand and shingle screening and grading plant, which was situated on what is known locally as the "Old Extension", officially referred to as the North Pier Extension. This is situated to the east of the Waveney Dock. Plans were first announced by the GER for the setting up of the plant in 1900. This plant was later replaced by a more substantial installation built by the LNER in the 1930s. Regular trains ran between the plant and the Harbour Works and for over 30 years the motive power used were the Sentinel designed Class Y1 and the Y3 0-4-0 tank locomotives. These historical views were recorded by the author on the 11th June 1957. The plant was demolished in 1960.
Left - This steam crane, one of several allocated to Lowestoft for departmental use, is seen removing shingle from the sea for processing at the plant.
Above - Standing on one of the many sidings at this very exposed location, while the crew take their tea break, is Civil Engineers Departmental Locomotive No. 38, a Class Y3 of 1927. Later, the truck seen coupled to the locomotive was loaded with graded sand and the locomotive returned with the truck to the town centre Harbour Works.

The plant in early February 1953 after the severe storms and associated flooding of the 31st January. Several wrecked trucks, some knocked off the lines by the power of the sea, and damaged sections of railway lines are evident.

A fine photograph taken from a glass plate negative showing, in the background, the first screening and grading plant built by the GER. Several Scottish herring drifters can be seen including, in the foreground, the Peterhead vessel *PD136 Promote*.

In February 1938 severe storms, which would be repeated in January 1953, caused great damage to the branch line leading to the plant. This damage cost over £40,000 to repair. The same sections of track were severely damaged again on the 31st January 1953. This photograph was taken on the 15th February 1938 and shows the smashed sea wall and, in the distance, one of the LNER steam cranes from the Harbour Works employed on track repairs.

Very few people witnessed the marvellous view from the top of the shingle screener and grader. Looking south, we see the dredger *Pioneer* working near the pier heads, and grounded GER coach bodies near the railway line leading to the harbour entrance. Also visible are the Claremont Pier and St. Luke's Hospital.

Lowestoft was the home to the last J. Holden designed Class F3 2-4-2 tank locomotive, a type which first entered service in 1893. Here we find the survivor, No. 67127, outside Lowestoft sheds which, in the 1950s, were re-roofed resulting in alterations being made to the end walls of the building. This locomotive regularly hauled the 10.00 am through train to York, complete with restaurant car, from Lowestoft to Reedham.

For a number of years in the mid 1950s, one example of another class of locomotive designed by J. Holden, the GER Class T26 2-4-0, later to become Class E4, was represented at Lowestoft. This locomotive, No. 62797, is seen here on shed on the 6th April 1957, with the fire being thrown out. It had just returned from a regular duty, that of shunting the yard at Halesworth and other stations on the East Suffolk line. In 1957 No. 62797 was withdrawn from service and left Lowestoft in July. This class was introduced in 1891. One example has been preserved, and is now part of the National Collection at York.

A view of the four road shed at Lowestoft, with Classes B17, L1, J67 and two 2-4-2 tank locomotives present. The original sheds were located adjacent to the station and were very small, with room for four locomotives. Complaints were received by the GER from residents living in the houses opposite the sheds about the smoke from locomotives. It was recommended in 1882 that larger sheds, at a new location, be built costing £5650 and it is these that are seen here. In the 1930s, new coal handling and water softening plants were installed. Closed in 1960, the sheds were demolished in 1983.

Visiting Class J39/1 0-6-0 No. 64724 being turned on the turntable at Lowestoft in 1957. No. 64724 was allocated to Ipswich shed and fitted with the standard 3500 gallon tender. It was withdrawn in February 1960. This turntable was situated on the south side of the shed building and replaced a smaller one, located further east. Areas containing sheds, turntable, water and coaling plants were often referred to as "Motive Power Depots". However, for convenience we have referred to these locations as "sheds", this being a time honoured and familiar expression to many.

After the Second World War the need to rebuild was paramount and new classes of locomotives appeared. One of these was the Thompson designed Class L1 2-6-4 tank locomotive and, in the 1950s, a number of these were allocated to Lowestoft shed (32C). A long time resident of 32C, No. 67704, is seen heading a Norwich train out of the town. As was quite normal procedure, fish vans have been attached to the passenger train. No. 67704 was transferred away from Lowestoft in January 1959.

Another of Lowestoft's L1s, No. 67770, is seen here on the morning of Sunday the 20th January 1957 collecting vans from the sidings to attach to a morning passenger departure. During July 1957 this locomotive was transferred away from Lowestoft. There were one hundred locomotives of this class built, designed by Edward Thompson for the LNER as a powerful mixed traffic locomotive.

The Class J15 0-6-0 general freight locomotives had a long association with Lowestoft and could be found undertaking all types of work from hauling the "Holiday Camps Express" to working on the Kirkley branch goods. Here we find No. 65478 involved in transfer work in the extensive sidings which Lowestoft once had. The date is the 11th June 1957. A splendid example of this type of locomotive has been preserved by the Midland & Great Northern Joint Railway Society and can usually be found at home on the highly acclaimed North Norfolk Railway.

Various types of GER 0-6-0 tank locomotives used for yard shunting and transfer work were very much part of the railway scene at Lowestoft. In the 1950s, two of these versatile locomotives could usually be found working daily in the sidings. Class J69/2 No. 68565 propels a train through the yard on the 8th June 1957.

Coke Ovens Junction Signal Box was situated at the junction of the Norfolk and Suffolk Joint Railways Committee's line to Yarmouth and what was originally the Norfolk Railway's Lowestoft to Reedham branch. The box is seen here, with the one time familiar sign indicating the direction and distance to Lowestoft. The origin of the name "Coke Ovens", is that the signal box was located close to where the ECR coke ovens were in the middle of the nineteenth century.

The morning of the 1st January 1957 finds Class F6 2-4-2T No. 67231 busy shunting, while Class D16/3 4-4-0 No. 62540 backs down from the sheds to pick up a train bound for Norwich. No. 62540 is one of the class with modified footplating.

As it waits in the sidings to depart with the afternoon fish train in the mid 1950s, Lowestoft allocated Gresley K3 2-6-0 No. 61959 is providing a traditional and, then, sadly declining service. Boxed fish has been brought from the market adjacent to the docks by lorry and is being loaded.

Other sidings equipped with loading platforms, are full of passenger stock indicating that times were changing in respect of the amount of goods and freight sent by rail.

Class F6 2-4-2T No. 67234 shunts empty fish vans into the loading platforms. By the time this scene was recorded, the great majority of fish landed at Lowestoft left the town in modern insulated and often refrigerated lorries with guaranteed delivery times direct to customers. As now, these were loaded with boxed fish at the fish market or the processing halls. This avoided the procedure described above whereby the merchants had to take the fish to the sidings, or sometimes the station, for sending by rail. Locally the lorry, which was cheaper and often faster, started to compete with rail after the First World War. By 1928 several local haulage firms were established in fish distribution.

Boxes of fish being loaded into a fish van from a lorry in the early 1950s at Lowestoft sidings.

In the early days, fish was sent from Lowestoft in open trucks loaded at the back of the market adjacent to the docks. Ironically this procedure was used for the last fish traffic to be carried by rail from the town. This was fish and fish offal, unfit for human consumption and used as animal feed. Dr. Ian Allen recorded diesel mechanical shunter Class 03 0-6-0 No. 2018 crossing the A12 trunk road with the daily two trucks of this material in 1970. This ceased in September 1973, other fish traffic having been lost to the lorry several years previously.

Locomotives of the Great Central Railway were represented locally by Class A5 4-6-2 tank locomotives. During the 1950s, three of this impressive class were allocated to Lowestoft shed. One of them, No. 69829, stands in Platform 3 at Lowestoft station waiting to depart with a Norwich train. These large tank locomotives were designed by J. G. Robinson for the Great Central and introduced in 1911. The three left Lowestoft in February 1957.

Note the extended canopy on the platform. Lowestoft now has a station where no protection from the elements exists on any platform.

Towards the end of steam working at Lowestoft, on the 7th February 1960, we find J15 0-6-0 No. 65462 stored at the shed. The bunker of former Norwich station pilot Class J50 0-6-0T 68924, also stored, is just visible, Outside the shed is one of the Lowestoft allocated Class B1 4-6-0s and in the background the front of the much respected Eastern Coach Works bus and coach factory which closed in 1987. No. 65462 was later purchased by the M&GN Railway Society for preservation. It can normally be seen on the North Norfolk Railway.

This unusual and finely detailed view of platform two at Lowestoft in 1953, shows Class F5 2-4-2T No. 67187 waiting to leave on a local stopping train. In the distance, on the left, can be seen the open external doors to the station concourse and to the right of them the doors of the refreshment rooms, well known for the large rail network map on the wall and fireplace with welcoming fires in the winter.

Looking across from platform three in 1956, we see Norwich allocated Class L1 2-6-4T No. 67714 and Class N7 0-6-2T No. 69706 waiting to proceed to Lowestoft sheds from platform two after working in with a train from Norwich. These types were well known locally with a number of examples allocated to Lowestoft shed. Both locomotives were transferred away from Norwich in 1957, No. 69706 finding a new home at Lowestoft.

A badly run down B17/6 No. 61670 *City of London* approaches the sheds at Lowestoft. In 1959, No. 61670 was allocated to Lowestoft to work East Suffolk line trains to London. *City of London* was withdrawn from service in April 1960 and scrapped at Stratford. The condition of the locomotive as seen here is very different from that in 1937, when it was one of two chosen to be streamlined and finished in apple green livery. No. 61670 was built by Robert Stephenson & Co. in 1937 under Works No. 4132. Originally named *Manchester City*, it later became *Tottenham Hotspur* and eventually, in 1937, *City of London*.

The Eastern Coach Works (ECW) at Lowestoft was very well known as a builder of high quality buses and coaches. However, in 1958 they received an order from British Railways for two lightweight railbuses for service in Scotland. Each chassis was produced by the Bristol Tramway & Carriage Co. Ltd. Built when attempts were being made to encourage the use of unprofitable rural railway lines, they were withdrawn in 1966. Here we see one of the pair in September 1962, complete with the familiar Bristol/ECW badge, at Beith on the branch line from Lugton.

This view, featuring Hunslet Class 05 0-6-0 diesel mechanical shunter No. D2570 at Lowestoft, contains many aspects of the area no longer seen. These include the sidings, the line leading to platform one (now the car park), the Railway Mission in Denmark Road, the fuel storage tanker used for refuelling locomotives and diesel multiple units and, just visible near the tanker, the cattle pens. Introduced in 1955, the Class 05 locomotive had a Gardner 8L3 engine developing 204bhp at 1200rpm. Diesel shunters took over from steam at Lowestoft in mid 1957.

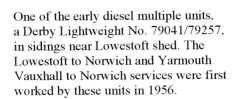

One of the early diesel multiple units, a Derby Lightweight No. 79041/79257, in sidings near Lowestoft shed. The Lowestoft to Norwich and Yarmouth Vauxhall to Norwich services were first worked by these units in 1956.

It is a fine autumn morning in 1957 at Woodbridge as we find Class B17/6 No. 61649 *Sheffield United* paused with a London to Lowestoft and Yarmouth stopping train. The locomotive, from Ipswich shed, is in fine external condition. No. 61649 entered service in 1936 as LNER No. 2849, becoming No. 1649 in 1946. *Sheffield United* became 61649 with nationalisation in 1948 and was withdrawn from service in February 1959. It was scrapped at Doncaster one month later.

The railway swing bridge is a well known feature of Oulton Broad. Class L1 2-6-4T No. 67704 rattles the bridge in May 1958, as it heads for Beccles with through carriages for London. The track at that time was double. With the modernisation of the East Suffolk line, the complete section between Oulton Broad North Junction and Halesworth was reduced to single track.

Left - The Sleeper Depot on the shores of Lake Lothing was an important Civil Engineers establishment in the town. The second of two such depots, both being established by the GER, it closed in 1964. The earlier depot was sold in 1917. This very interesting view taken from a footbridge adjacent to Lake Lothing shows the depot on the right. Track relaying is in progress on the main running lines. A Class J17 0-6-0, working wrong line, is with the permanent way train.

Above - Introduced in the 1920s, chain driven steam Civil Engineers Departmental Locomotives designed by the Sentinel Wagon Co. worked at the depot. Two of these are seen here amongst the stacks of sleepers.

Above Left - Class Y1/1 No. 37
Above Right - Class Y3 No. 40.

One fascinating aspect of the Sleeper Depot was the narrow gauge railway there. The author worked at the depot in 1958 and 1959, and spent time inspecting this three-foot gauge locomotive, used for propelling trucks containing sleepers into the pressurised creosoting chambers at the depot.

The locomotive displayed no name, but LNER No. 3 was visible together with a totem sign proclaiming "British Railways". One other small narrow gauge locomotive was on site at that time. A number of steam cranes were based in the depot. In the foreground can be seen dual gauge track, with three-foot gauge inside the standard gauge track.

The date is the 17th September 1958.

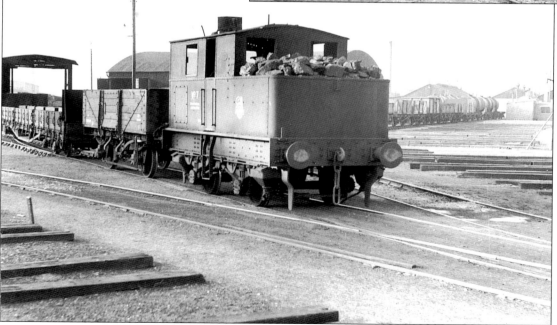

This view of the depot by Dr. Ian Allen shows Sentinel Departmental Locomotive No.7 at work in the yard. The old sleepers set in the ground either side of No. 7 would normally be covered by stacks around 20ft. high, of new sleepers in the process of being seasoned. The depot closed in 1964, the land later being used by Shell UK for offices, a helipad, supply ship berths and stores complex.

From Lowestoft a large amount of goods and fish traffic, in addition to a diverse timetable of through trains, passed through Yarmouth Beach station. In fact, at one time, it was considered very much a major route out of Lowestoft. In this view of the yard at Beach station we see LMS Ivatt 2-6-0 No. 43107 preparing to leave with a goods train.

The versatile Ivatt 4MT locomotives were very much the mainstay of motive power on the former M&GN lines in the 1950s when this scene was recorded. One example of the class, No. 43106, has been preserved and can be found on the Severn Valley Railway. This locomotive was a frequent visitor to Yarmouth Beach.

A fascinating scene at a location which is now very well known as a Pitch & Putt course and the Pleasurewood Hills Family Theme Park. Class D16/3 4-4-0 No. 62596 heads south towards Lowestoft in August 1957 with empty coaching stock on the line between Lowestoft and Yarmouth. Of this superb scene, only the bridge now remains, heavily vandalised. Locally there is a strong feeling that this line should never have closed. Vast housing estates have been built between the two towns, in addition to the District Hospital, all within easy walking distance of the now vanished line and stations

Another view of the line between Lowestoft and Yarmouth. Class B1 4-6-0 No. 61233 approaches Hopton-on-Sea station with a through express working from London Liverpool Street, via Lowestoft. This area is now covered by housing; the only evidence that the railway ever existed being former railway houses and a gate. This and other stations on the line, were the holiday destinations for hundreds of people over many years.

Another of the versatile Class B1 4-6-0 locomotives designed by Edward Thomson and introduced in 1942. No. 61372 heads south with an up freight from Lowestoft on the East Suffolk line near Halesworth in August 1960. Lowestoft shed officially closed to steam locomotives the following month. No. 61372 was allocated to Parkeston shed at the time.

The Lowestoft South Branch was a very important part of the complex rail networks of Lowestoft. One section of the main line of the branch ran parallel to, and between, Notley Road and Kimberley Road. This is where Dr. Ian Allen recorded Class J15 0-6-0 No. 65478 in the 1950s, returning to the junction at Oulton Broad South. In steam days the usual motive power to be seen on the branch were either Class J15 or J17 0-6-0s.

Over twenty years later and the branch continues to provide a service to the many customers it served. Some of the last major users of the line were the Cooperative Wholesale Society, with large consignments of oil for the factory boilers, Brooke Marine shipyard, with deliveries of steel, and Boulton & Paul with timber products. Class 03 0-6-0 No.D2155 is seen trundling along the branch with steel for Brooke Marine not long before the branch closed in 1972. Houses in Victoria Road are in the background.

Far Left - The junction at Oulton Broad South with the branch to the right of the signal box, and the line to Lowestoft Central on the left. Centre Left - Colville Road level crossing after removal of the gates. The track bed behind the young lady is now occupied by housing. Below - Adjacent to Notley Road level crossing, Class J15 No. 65389 is on the Kirkley Goods Yard line, with the South Quay line to the left of the J15. On the far left, Class J17 No. 65559 is on the line leading to several sites including Brooke Marine, Boulton & Paul and the Cooperative Wholesale Society.

The last locomotive hauled through train from London to Lowestoft ran in 1984. Class 37 Co-Co diesel electric locomotives were the usual motive power provided for these trains in both directions for over twenty years. On arrival at Lowestoft in the evening, it was usual for the locomotive to take empty newspaper vans to Norwich, the stock of the through train being stabled and cleaned at Lowestoft. During the 1960s, the locomotive also remained overnight at Lowestoft, stabled with the diesel shunters. With a Class 03 0-6-0 shunter having drawn the coaching stock out of platform four, No. 37017 prepares to leave with the vans on the 9th June 1980.

In recent years six different types of diesel electric locomotives, classes 31, 37, 47, 56, 66, and 67, have departed from Lowestoft with freight trains on the first stage of their journey to Aberdeen. Three types are featured here, the others are to be found elsewhere in this book. Class 31 locomotives, including No. 31142 worked a few of these trains, one of which was on the 9th October 1998. The locomotive is seen running round the train prior to departure.

Displaying the early English, Welsh and Scottish Railway livery, Class 37 Co-Co No. 37682 Hartlepool Pipe Mill departs from Lowestoft in December 1998, with another train for Aberdeen.

A busy time at Lowestoft on the 2nd December 1999, with two trains in the yard. The empty one has just arrived behind Class 56 Co-Co No. 56060, while a loaded train awaits collection by the Class 56. Introduced in 1976, the Class 56 is powered by a 16cyl GEC engine developing 3250bhp, and is very rarely seen at Lowestoft. Some of these locomotives were built in Romania, and others in the UK.

The Great Eastern Railway and other railway companies did much to develop the harbour and invested vast amounts of money in the infrastructure. It is likely that, without the substantial railway backing over many years, the harbour at Lowestoft would not exist today. This postcard ensures that everybody knows who owned the port of Lowestoft. The trucks conveying salt and barrels illustrate two important items supplied to the then great fishing industry.

THE FISH MARKETS, LOWESTOFT.
The property of the Great Eastern Railway Company.

Initially the harbour was not built with the fishing industry in mind. However it soon became involved in one of Britain's biggest fisheries. Large numbers of Scottish and English fishing vessels crowd the North Quay at Lowestoft to land vast quantities of fish into open railway wagons during a glut in herring landings. The fish were destined for processing into meal for agricultural purposes. Unfortunately for the fishermen, scenes such as this meant their labours at sea were not well rewarded. At Yarmouth trains of around 60 trucks left the town for the meal factories, the fish juices and blood dripping from the train as it travelled through the town from the fish wharf.

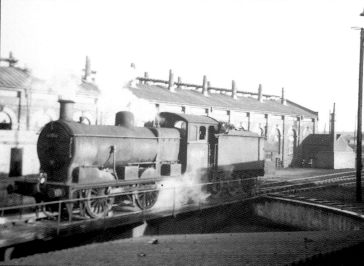

Bottom Left - One of the last visits to Lowestoft by a former GER locomotive was on New Years Eve in 1960, when Class J17 0-6-0 No. 65586 visited the closed Lowestoft sheds to turn, prior to working a special children's Christmas train to Yarmouth.

The last recorded steam hauled train left Lowestoft in 1962. However, it was not long before steam locomotives again appeared in the town. For a number of years Class B1 4-6-0's were allocated to Lowestoft in the winter months to provide steam heating for hauled stock prior to departure behind diesel locomotives. Other locations where the B1s were allocated for this work included Norwich, Ipswich and Yarmouth Vauxhall. The locomotives were rotated to allow a boiler wash out to take place whilst working at Norwich.

Top Left - It has often been stated in railway books and magazines that these locomotives, whilst employed on heating duties, had their screw couplings removed. This photograph, taken by the author on the 9th February 1965, proves that at least No. 61138 still retained screw couplings whilst at Lowestoft.

Top Right - A fine view of Class B1 4-6-0 No. 61204 as Departmental Locomotive No. 19 at Lowestoft on the 21st February 1965.

Many unusual and special charter trains have visited Lowestoft in recent years. Examples of these are featured here.

The working on the 24th August 1999 was unusual in that the train arrived behind Class 37s No. 37713 and 37513 and left hauled by Class 31s No D5528 and 31154. After running round, the Class 37s are seen propelling the train into platform four.

British Rail failed to give a good impression to hundreds of American visitors travelling to Lowestoft on the *Orient Express* in April 1989. The train, seen here, was hauled by a very dirty Class 47 No. 47657, and on arrival at platform four they were greeted by the long grass and weeds growing there.

On the 29th August 2000, the exceptionally clean Class 47 No. 47736 *Cambridge* arrives with the stock for a long distance charter, provided by a major multinational company for its local staff. The train consisted of Rail Charter Services BN93 luxury set, the *Pride of the Nation*. Bringing up the rear of the train was an equally clean Class 47 No. 47776 *Respected*.

A steam hauled train from London was due to visit Lowestoft on the 10th November 2001, but unfortunately the locomotive failed at Norwich. This resulted in the train being hauled by Class 67 diesel locomotive No. 67024 to Lowestoft and then back to London. The late running train is seen here at Haddiscoe with the Class 67 putting on a fine performance.

For various reasons, on a number of occasions, local service trains have been replaced by locomotive hauled stock. Class 47 Co-Co No. 47715 *Haymarket* waits to leave Norwich with the Lowestoft train. It is displaying the Network SouthEast livery which was rarely seen locally. In recent years Anglia Railways have been praised for the way they consistently attempt to maintain normal services and overcome the many difficulties, encountered in operating a train service in the twenty-first century.

PHOTOGRAPHIC INDEX

PHOTOGRAPHS ON BACK COVER

Top Left - Norwich allocated Class K3 2-6-0 No. 61953 approaches Oulton Broad with the York to Lowestoft through coaches in September 1958.

Top Right - On the 8th April 2002, EWS Class 66 No. 66045 passes the site of the original Haddiscoe station whilst heading a freight from Lowestoft.

Bottom Left - Yarmouth Southtown allocated Class D16/3 4-4-0 No. 62546 Claud Hamilton is seen here in May 1956 at Southtown shed. It was withdrawn from service in June 1957, but had been a frequent visitor to Lowestoft whilst working Yarmouth services.

Bottom Right - Fragonset Railways Class 31 No. 31468 Hydra returns to Norwich with the stock of a Lowestoft Air Show shuttle on the 4th August 2000.